IMAGES OF
America

GENERATIONS
OF BLACK LIFE
IN KENNESAW AND MARIETTA
GEORGIA

Bishop Henry McNeal Turner was the first black appointed U.S. Army chaplin and Georgia legislator during reconstruction. He pastored churches in Kennesaw and Marietta, Georgia. (Courtesy of Moorland-Spingran Research Center, Howard University.)

Cover Image: Lemon Street, the first black public elementary school in Marietta, opened its door in 1894. Pictured here is the second principal of the school, Luke B. Norris (top right, standing), with his seventh grade graduating class. (Courtesy of Powerpointe Archives.)

IMAGES OF
America

GENERATIONS
OF BLACK LIFE
IN KENNESAW AND MARIETTA
GEORGIA

Patrice Shelton Lassiter

Foreword by Juliet Dobbs Blackburn-Beamon, D.A.

ARCADIA

Published by Arcadia Publishing,
an imprint of Tempus Publishing, Inc.
2 Cumberland Street
Charleston, SC 29401

Printed in Great Britain.

Library of Congress Catalog Card Number: Applied for.

For all general information contact Arcadia Publishing at:
Telephone 843-853-2070
Fax 843-853-0044
E-Mail arcadia@charleston.net

For customer service and orders:
Toll-Free 1-888-313-BOOK

Visit us on the internet at http://www.arcadiaimages.com

Dedication

I dedicate this book to my mother, Ursula Hall Shelton, for her support and encouragement; my brother, Bradley D. Shelton, for his insight and spiritual guidance. A special dedication goes to my husband and friend, Brian E. Lassiter, for giving me unending support throughout all my endeavors; and my daughter, Nia Marie Lassiter, who will build upon this knowledge of family and community with the understanding of who we were, who we are, and who we've yet to become.

John Wesley Dobbs, Atlanta civic leader, was born in Kennesaw in 1882. (Courtesy of Juliet Dobbs Blackburn-Beamon, DA.)

CONTENTS

FOREWORD

People, places, and time are the "stuff" of history, and here we have an unusual amalgamation of many of those things from the black past of Cobb County, Georgia.

Can you picture rural north Georgia around 1880? If not, come along on this journey via the town of Marietta and come round the mountain called Kennesaw where we'll all go out and meet the train as did the forgotten (or never-known) black folk of that early history. These were key settlements of that time, and the lives, activities, hopes, and beliefs of their black inhabitants were key to, not only their development, but ultimately, Atlanta.

Mired in the mud of the records of that period are stories and the real truths that reveal the culture of actually more than one group of forgotten Americans. The realities and relationships among the Native Americans, freed slaves, and mulattos are revealed in Mrs. Lassiter's sensitive photo-narrative. Also, it is her unusual combination of strategic and search skills that have made possible the discovery of facts in obscure records that, most often, would go unrecognized. Add to this her ability to go beyond the point where most researchers would put the period, and we truly find ourselves on a train ride to truth and inspiration.

In this charming photo-history, Patrice Shelton Lassiter also highlights unexpected connections of black people in Marietta and Kennesaw to the development of their sister city to the south, Marthasville. Destined to later become (because of that very same railroad) the next great international city of our world, Atlanta owes much of its heritage to surprising contributions of pivotal black leaders fostered by these towns. These include formidable men of vision and fortitude like Henry McNeal Turner, Hamp Jackson, John Wesley Dobbs, and Maynard Holbrook Jackson Jr. "Quite a journey" you say? Come with me!

—Juliet Dobbs Blackburn-Beamon, DA
Granddaughter of John Wesley Dobbs

INTRODUCTION

In metropolitan Atlanta, there are two cities approximately 15-20 miles from downtown. Interstate 75 North will take you to Marietta and Kennesaw, Georgia. Minutes from each other, these cities make up a part of Cobb County, one of the fastest-growing counties in the United States. The growth experienced in Atlanta during the 1970s and '80s simultaneously sparked development in the nearby cities of Marietta and Kennesaw. Today, corporations, subdivisions, and shopping malls take the place of what were once rural farm communities. The days of horse-drawn carriages and cotton as the major source of agriculture have vanished forever.

Marietta and Kennesaw were like many Southern towns after the ending of slavery in 1865. Southern Blacks soon realized that freedom did not mean equality. The year slavery ended, Pres. Andrew Johnson permitted the establishment of the Black Codes, which limited the rights of blacks. The Black Codes intended to "re-establish slavery under another name." The continuation of two separate Souths, a "White South" and a "Black South," existed for more than 100 years after slavery ended.

Although there were racial divisions and inequities in the South, black communities were able to survive and develop institutions, many of which continue today. The black church took on a new meaning and expression after slavery. The church was the first place that blacks could freely express themselves and worship without the supervision of the white church. The majority of traditional Southern black churches were established by the late 1880s and became the center for religious and social gatherings. Additionally, the black church provided a meeting place for the community and its leadership to discuss and plan strategies on political issues that affected them.

The first elementary educational system for black children in the South originated in the black churches. In the late 1890s, segregated public school systems in Georgia would only offer an elementary education to black children. The first black high schools that opened in most cities in the South were usually the results of joint efforts between black teachers, the black community, and philanthropic donations from Northerners.

Black people have been in Marietta and Kennesaw since the formation of the Cobb County seat in 1832; however, it wasn't until after slavery ended that these new communities emerged. In spite of a continued system of segregation and discrimination in the South, black people in both cities worked hard to build churches, schools, and, for the first time, strong family and community ties.

A unique relationship existed between blacks in Marietta and Kennesaw. It was not uncommon to see people from both communities working together. Religious and social gatherings were held in Kennesaw at the popular black country club "King's Wigwam" in the early 1900s. Both communities would gather there for baptisms, picnics, and dances. Family members in Marietta and Kennesaw would visit back and forth on weekends and special occasions. Children from Kennesaw would travel to Marietta by horse and buggy, and later by truck and bus, to the only secondary "colored" school in the surrounding areas, Lemon Street.

You may ask, why a pictorial history on the black communities of Marietta and Kennesaw, Georgia? My response would be "why isn't there any documentation or books on black life in Marietta or Kennesaw between 1865 and 1965?" This question could be asked with respect to many cities in the South before 1965. Segregated history excluded blacks from being written about other than as references to slavery.

Even after Sarah Gobler Temple wrote the book on the history of Cobb County, *The First Hundred Years*, which was not written until 1932, only a limited amount of information concerning black life is found in the index section under "Slavery." The author left out approximately 65 years of post-slavery history and development of black people in Kennesaw and Marietta. In his study "Cobb County, Georgia, 1880-1900: A Socioeconomic Study Of An Upper Piedmont County," Thomas Allan Scott examines the local newspaper *The Marietta Journal*, and its attitudes towards blacks during this time period as objects of humor and frequent ridicule.

Another important reason for this book is that the documentation of black life in the South at the turn of the 19th century through the first half of the 20th century is still very rare. As the older generations pass on, their family histories and pictures are being lost, sometimes even thrown away by those who don't understand their value.

Descendants of black families from Kennesaw and Marietta can be found in the Atlanta metropolitan area today. John Wesley Dobbs credited his early life in Kennesaw for much of his later accomplishments. John settled in Atlanta and became one of the original directors of the first black banks—Citizens Trust Bank, the Grand Master of the Masons, and, most notably, he organized and led the Atlanta Negro Voters League. He also worked closely with Thurgood Marshall in an effort to raise money for the NAACP. John Wesley Dobbs was the grandfather of the first black mayor of Atlanta, Maynard H. Jackson Jr., who resides in Atlanta today.

Other influential descendants from Kennesaw and Marietta are people like Juanita Byrd, who was the granddaughter of one of the founding fathers of Sardis Baptist Church, which was started in 1880. Mrs. Byrd continues her family's tradition along with her husband, Pastor Byrd, who is the associate pastor of the same church started by her grandfather over 110 years ago. Also, Bridgett Eppinger Greene is the third generation to work in the family business started by her grandfather and grandmother 70 years ago. Started on Cole Street in Marietta, Mack Eppinger's Funeral Home still serves the black residents of Kennesaw, Marietta, and Cartersville.

My discovery of six generations of Jackson ancestors on my mother's side inspired me to write this book. My family "roots," which include documented Cherokee ancestry, date back to the 1870s in both cities. A total of 120 years of my family history has taken place less than 35 miles away from the place where I grew up. At the turn of the 20th century, my great-great-grandfather owned many acres of land in Kennesaw, voted, and educated all of his children. My great-great-great-uncles invested "monies" in stocks with the Mutual Aid & Loan Investment Company. My great-grandfather was a skilled stone-cutter who voted and owned property.

As a graduate of Spelman College in Atlanta, Georgia, and descendant of former graduates of Spelman, Morris Brown, Morehouse, and Clark Colleges, it is with great pride that I present the first pictorial history on the black communities of Kennesaw and Marietta, Georgia. This book is only the beginning of what I hope will lead to additional research into the history of these two communities.

One
BEGINNINGS

Depicted here is the Southern Cherokee Delegation to Washington in 1866. From left to right are John Rollin Ridge, Saladin Watie, Richard Fields, E.C. Boudinot, and W.P. Adair.

In 1835, the Ridge-Waite-Boudinot Group (Cherokee leadership) along with the support of Cherokee chief John Ross (a mixed-blood Cherokee of mostly Scottish ancestry—not pictured) signed the treaty of New Echota with commissioners of the United States. In this treaty it was agreed that the Cherokees would cede their lands east of the Mississippi, including Georgia, and join the Cherokees to the west. In spite of overwhelming protest by the Cherokee people, the treaty was promptly ratified by the Senate, and, in 1838, the majority of Cherokees were forcefully removed to what is now Oklahoma.

Kennesaw and Marietta marked their beginnings on the displacement and removal of the majority of Cherokee people from their homeland. Georgia's Land and Gold Lotteries were held to disperse Cherokee lands to white males over 18 years of age, who were citizens of the United States and had lived in the State of Georgia for three years. Encroachment by white settlers on Cherokee lands was being upheld by Georgia laws. Despite the Supreme Court of the United States ruling on the unconstitutionality of these laws, Georgia pressed forward with their Land and Gold Lotteries.

On December 3, 1832, the Georgia Legislature passed the act providing for the organization of Cobb County. Marietta was the name selected for the county seat permanently incorporated on land lot 1218, District 16, and Kennesaw became a part of the District 20, second section of Cobb County. In the distribution of land in Kennesaw and Acworth there were 342 lots drawn. Marietta had 931 lots drawn in its Gold Lottery.

Early records indicate that Cobb County had 381 slaves in 1838. In 1845, the number of slaves in Cobb County rose to 1,474, and, in 1850, 2,272 were listed as slaves and 3 were listed as free colored persons. The need for slave labor increased in Cobb County as the white farmers set out to compete in the cotton market. In 1860, the slave population in Marietta was 1,175, and the number of free persons of color totaled 13. The few free blacks were put under such legal restrictions that they were not treated much better than the slaves themselves.

Enslaved people were mostly of African ancestry, yet many black families in Marietta and Kennesaw give oral and written accounts of Native American and/or European ancestry. After 1865, census classifications of blacks and "People of Color" in both areas were limited to two categories: mulatto, which usually denoted a mixture of African and European, and black, which referred to people of African descent. Persons with mixed African and Native American ancestries were probably classified as mulattos. Most early classifications of blacks represented the census takers' point of view, and in many instances the rich diversity of these two black communities were left out of historical records.

The Civil War gave freed black men and runaway slaves an opportunity to fight for the abolishment of slavery in the South. Marietta mentions in one of its newspapers, the *Chattanooga Daily Rebel*, dated October 22, 1863, a reward of $250 offered by local slave owners J. Tucker, J. Wood, and J.F. Rogers for the apprehension of five slaves. The slaves were said to have taken double-barreled shotguns and were trying to make their way to East Tennessee, the location of the Union Army forces. The ending of the Civil War in 1865 marked a new beginning for 3,304 freed blacks in Cobb County, Georgia.

Pictured on the left is Judge John Gann, office of ordinary, Cobb County *c.* 1910. Judge Gann's family were among white settlers who drew land in Cobb County from the lottery. The 1851 tax digest listed the elder John Gann as the owner of five slaves and 380 acres of land. (Courtesy of the Georgia Department of Archives and History.)

Mr. and Mrs. Gaspard T. Carrie are shown here in front of their home in Kennesaw c. 1870. Gaspard T. Carrie's father, Joseph Carrie, was the original drawer in the land lottery of 1832. Ben H. Carrie, son of Mr. and Mrs. Gaspard T. Carrie, became Marietta's Justice of the Peace in the early 1900s. (Courtesy of the Georgia Department of Archives and History.)

Sam Reynolds, a slave owned by Homer Reynolds of Cobb County, is seen here around 1864. (Courtesy of the Georgia Department of Archives and History.)

The expression "Cotton was King in the South" is seen in this picture of cotton farmers in Marietta, c. 1890, looking to get a fair price for their crops. (Courtesy of Hardy Studio, Marietta, Georgia.)

Mr. Alfred Lowe sits in front of his old home on what is now known as Bells Ferry Road. A former slave, Mr. Lowe, migrated to Kennesaw at the end of the Civil War. He worked and purchased many acres of land, a portion of which are still presently owned by his daughter, Mrs. Candice Hutchins. (Courtesy of Alfred Jackson.)

Maria Braxton Woodward, seen here *c.* 1890, and her daughter, Louella Woodward Patterson, arrived in Marietta, Georgia, in 1887. The granddaughter of former French-Native American-African slaves, Maria worked as a cook to help educate her daughter, Louella, who became one of Cobb County's first black women to attend college. (Courtesy of John W. Patterson.)

John and Anna Patterson, shown here c. 1880, arrived in Marietta around the late 1860s from South Carolina. Descendants of Native American/African parentage, they purchased property on Montgomery Street and operated one of the first restaurants in the black community. (Courtesy of John W. Patterson.)

Unidentified black women are washing clothes in Kennesaw, *c.* 1890. (Courtesy of the Georgia Department of Archives and History.)

Several cotton pickers are seen here getting their cotton weighted in Cobb County, *c.* 1900. (Courtesy of the Georgia Department of Archives and History.)

Two
BISHOP HENRY
MCNEAL TURNER
Laying the Foundation

Henry McNeal Turner is credited for organizing African Methodist Episcopal (AME) churches, Colored Methodist Episcopal churches, and influencing Black Baptist churches throughout the South. Though a bishop in the AME Church, his influence transcended denominations. Stephen Ward Angel, in his book *Bishop Henry McNeal Turner and African-American Religion in the South*, examines Bishop Turner as "one of the most skillful denominational builders in American History." Pictured here in his Episcopal robes, *c.* 1898, Henry McNeal Turner was a bishop in the AME Church from 1880 to 1915, a politician and Georgia legislator during Reconstruction, a U.S. Army chaplin, a newspaper editor, a prohibition advocate, a civil rights and Back-to-Africa advocate, an African missionary, the Chancellor of Morris Brown College, and an early proponent of Black Theology. (Courtesy of Moorland-Spingarn Research Center, Howard University.)

Geo. R. Gibson,   State of Georgia.
    To   Cobb County.
Rev. H. M. Turner   In Consideration of the
                 sum of Three hun-
dred Dollars ($300.) to me paid I, Geo.
R. Gibson of the County of Cobb, do hereby
sell and convey unto Henry M. Turner
of the County of Fulton, heirs and assigns.
a tract or parcel of land which is
described as follows. Forty acres, more or
less, out of the North East Corner of lot of
land number (129). One hundred & twenty Nine,
in the 20th District, and 2d Section of Cobb
County. bounded as follows, to wit, on the
North West by Western & Atlantic Railroad,
on North East by lands of H. M. Turner, on the
South & South East by Shila road, and on
West to lands of R. McFramling. & being
the same 40 acres, as described in deed
of J. F. Gibson, admr. of J. S. Gibson to Nancy
H. Gibson of date December 4" 1883.

To have and to hold said land and
appurtenances unto said H. M. Turner, his
heirs, executors, administrators, and assigns
in fee simple.
I warrant the title to said land against
the lawful claims of all persons.
In Witness Whereof, I have hereunto set my
hand & affixed my seal, this 24" day of
December, 1888.
Signed Sealed & Delivered
   In presence of   Geo. R. Gibson
   John D. White,
   W. R. Montgomery. C/c.

Recorded, this Jany 4/89. W. R. Montgomery c/c.

Jno. B. Kendrick   State of Georgia.
    To   Cobb County.
Lemuel C. Harris.   This Indenture
                 made & entered
into this 16" day of December in the year
of Our Lord, One thousand Eight hundred
and, Eighty Eight, between John B. Kendrick
of the County of Cobb, of the first part, and
Lemuel C. Harris, of the County of Cobb of
the Second part, Witnesseth, That the said
party of the first part, for and in consideration of the sum of One hundred Dollars,
in hand paid, at and before the sealing

Deed records show that Rev. Henry McNeal Turner purchased 40 acres of land in April 1889 in Kennesaw, District 20, second section of Cobb County. Between 1865 and 1867, Henry McNeal Turner became the first minister of Mt. Zion AME Church in Kennesaw and the first black minister of Turner Chapel AME Church in Marietta. In 1867, he brought both congregations into their first annual African Methodist Episcopal Conference. He maintained a residence in Kennesaw for many years. The land where the "Old Turner House" stood can still be seen today.

Henry McNeal Turner's contribution to the extension of the AME Church into Africa is shown here in this rare photograph, c. 1898, at the Transvaal Annual Conference in Pretoria, South Africa. He organized four annual conferences in Africa; Sierra Leone, Liberia, Pretoria, and Queenstown. Turner is seated on the second row, fifth from the left. (Courtesy of Moorland-Spingarn Research Center, Howard University.)

Pictured here is Henry McNeal Turner with two unidentified men who bare a striking resemblance to him. Henry was born in South Carolina on February 1, 1834, to Sarah and Hardy Turner. He was raised by his mother and maternal grandmother. His father died while he was still a child. Born a free person and grandson of an African prince, Henry's childhood was spent working side-by-side with slaves. At the age of 12, Henry experienced a dream that led him to believe he would become a leader and teacher for large masses of people. He later became one of the most influential ministers/bishops in the African Methodist Episcopal Church. (Courtesy of Moorland-Spingarn Research Center, Howard University.)

Right: Turner's mother, Sarah Greer Turner Story, hired several whites to teach her son, only to have other whites threaten to expose them, as it was illegal for whites to assist in the education of blacks. (Courtesy of Moorland-Spingarn Research Center, Howard University.) *Left:* Eliza Peacher Turner was Henry McNeal Turner's first wife. Henry and Eliza had 14 children. This picture dates from around 1890.

Right: Martha Elizabeth Dewitt Turner, seen here *c.* 1900, was Henry McNeal Turner's second wife. *Left:* Harriet Wayman Turner was Henry's third wife.

SPEECH

ON THE

ELIGIBILITY OF COLORED MEMBERS
To Seats

In the Georgia Legislature.

By Hon. H. M. TURNER,

(Colored.)

Delivered before that Body September 3d, 1868.

Mr. Speaker:

Before proceeding to argue this question upon its intrinsic merits, I wish the Members of this House to understand the position that I take. I hold that I am a member of this body. Therefore, sir, I shall neither fawn nor cringe before any party, nor stoop to *beg* them for my rights. Some of my colored fellow-members, in the course of their remarks, took occasion to appeal to the *sympathies* of Members on the opposite side, and to eulogize their character for magnanimity. It reminds me very much, sir, of slaves begging under the lash. I am here to demand my rights, and to hurl thunderbolts at the men who would dare to cross the threshold of my manhood. There is an old aphorism which says, "Fight the Devil with fire," and if I should observe the rule in this instance, I wish gentlemen to understand that it is but fighting them with their own weapon.

The scene presented in this House, to-day, is one unparalleled in the history of the world. From this day, back to the day when God breathed the breath of life into Adam, no analogy for it can be found. Never, in the history of the world, has a man been arraigned before a body clothed with legislative, judicial or executive functions, charged with the offence of being of a darker hue than his fellow-men. I know that questions have been before the Courts of this country, and of other

This speech, delivered by Henry McNeal Turner on September 3, 1868, changed the course of history for black legislators in Georgia. With great oratorical skill and intellect, Henry McNeal Turner successfully defended the rights of the black legislators to hold their seats. In 1874, Turner led a delegation of 400 blacks on a 20-mile march to Effinham County, Georgia, in order to protect the rights of black voters. He sought support for a federal civil rights bill in 1872 as well as encouraging black people to consider going back to Africa because of continuing violence by whites against Southern blacks. Fifty years later, Marcus Garvey, leader of the UNIA, popularized the Back-to-Africa Movement and Black Nationalism advocated by Henry McNeal Turner. Today, a large portrait of Congressman Turner hangs in the Georgia State Capital Building in Atlanta. Other monuments include the Turner Theological Seminary and Museum located at the Atlanta University Center and Turner Henry McNeal Middle School and Turner Henry McNeal High School located on Anderson Street in Atlanta.

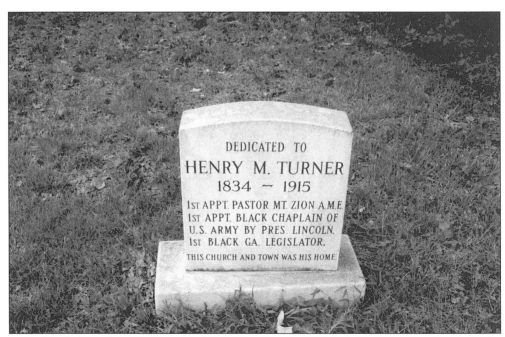

A marker dedicated to Turner sits behind Mt. Zion AME Church located in Kennesaw in the century-and-a-half-old cemetery.

Three
CHURCH AND RELIGION
The Foundation

Mr. and Mrs. Leonard are dressed for church service, in Cobb County *c.* 1880. The center of black life in Kennesaw and Marietta was the Church. Before 1865, most churches had integrated congregations with segregated policies toward its black members. As a result of these inequalities, blacks began to establish separate churches around the late 1860s through the early 1870s. (Courtesy of Juanita Byrd and Powerpointe Archives.)

Pictured here under the pastorate of Rev. J.M. Lee is the congregation of Zion Baptist Church in front of the old church building on Haynes and Lemon Streets in Marietta, c. 1935. In 1991, the oldest Black Baptist church in Marietta, Zion Baptist was entered into the National Registry of Historical Places. (Courtesy of the Georgia Department of Archives and History.)

In 1865, a black delegation from First Baptist Church in Marietta applied for letters of dismissal in order to form a separate and distinct body from the white First Baptist Church. In 1866, First Baptist Church granted letters of dismissal to 89 black members. On April 8, 1866, Zion Baptist Church was formally organized under the leadership of Rev. Ephraim B. Rucker. Pictured here, c. 1935, is Old Zion Baptist, built in 1888 during the pastorate of Rev. C.G. Holmes. In 1978, Zion Baptist opened a new church building located across the street from the old church. (Courtesy of Powerpointe Archives.)

Old Noonday Baptist Church in Kennesaw was founded in the 1880s. Pictured here, c. 1920, are Mr. and Mrs. Hutchins standing in front of the old church. Mrs. Hutchins is the daughter of one of Kennesaw's early black residents, Mr. Alfred Lowe. (Alfred Jackson and Powerpointe Archives.)

Sardis Baptist Church in Kennesaw, seen here c. 1890, was founded in 1880 by Deacon Stephen Jack Talley, Deacon Sam Bostic, and Deacon Alexander James Tanner. The members of Sardis recall it being referred to as the "Colored Baptist Church," because it was assumed to be the only black church in Kennesaw at that time. Church history talks of black folks coming to Kennesaw to take advantage of job opportunities on the Western & Atlantic Railway. Sardis' history recalls Sunday-morning services offering standing room only because of the large congregations. (Juanita Byrd and Powerpointe Archives.)

Deacon Tanner, born in 1865, was one of the founding fathers of "Old Sardis Baptist Church." Deacon Tanner was found burned to death on April 15, 1940. Mr. Tanner was an outspoken and respected leader in the community and his death still remains a mystery within the black community. He is pictured here standing in front of the original church building that was destroyed by fire in 1930. (Juanita Byrd and Powerpointe Archives.)

Pictured here is Deacon Tanner in the mid-1930s. He married Emma Strickland Tanner and they had nine daughters. (Courtesy of Juanita Byrd.)

Pictured here, c. 1920, is the actual notification of the rally that was held by Sardis Baptist Church to raise money to rebuild the church after it was destroyed by fire. (Courtesy of Juanita Byrd.)

The Sardis Baptist Church
Kennesaw, Ga.

Grand $1.000 Rally

This money is for the rebuilding of the church, that must be done at once. The church has appointed ten Clubs, each $100.

The Rally will come off the 5th Sunday in October, 1920.

CLUB CAPTAINS

Mrs. Emma Talley
"   "   Tanner
"   Georgia Howel
"   Alleta Paiten
"   Anthany Knox
"   Dovie Humphries
"   Sara Miller
"   Dulley
"   Lucile Macafee
"   Willie Austin

Also Mrs. Saphronia Knox, of Birmingham, Ala.

All Day Meeting, Refreshments on the grounds.

The following Churches are invited:

Coal St. Marietta Ga.,	Rev. Dr. L. J. Wilders, Pastor
Liberty Hill	" S. Henry, "
Noonday	" Maxey "
Zion A. M. E.	" Zelos "
Zion, Actworth	" W. J. White "

Come and help us, we thank you.

THE CHURCH, KENNESAW, GA.
REV. Wm. T. JOHNSON, Pastor.,
164 E. Cain St. Atlanta, Ga.

Mrs. Saphronia Knox and her husband came all the way from Birmingham, Alabama, to assist in efforts to raise money to rebuild Sardis Baptist Church. Mrs. Knox is listed as one of the club captains for the fund-raising event c. 1920. (Courtesy of Juanita Byrd.)

After the original Sardis Baptist Church was destroyed by fire, members and friends in the community worked together to build the new church, pictured here, which was completed in 1945, under the pastorate of Rev. L.M. Buggs.

Reverend Davenport was instrumental in starting the youth choir and junior choir during his pastorate at Sardis Baptist Church. He is pictured here performing a baptism c. 1930. (Courtesy of Claudia McGuire.)

Referred to as the black country club resort during the turn of the century, King's Wigwam was used for church baptisms, picnics, and other events. A large building stood on this 40-acre resort that accommodated a variety of activities. The King's Wigwam is said to have been owned by Bishop Henry NcNeal Turner, who named it after his daughter, Victoria Turner King, who died in childbirth in 1892. Others believe that the resort was owned by an Atlantan, David T. Howard, who was a black businessman and the only black undertaker at that time.

The King's Wigwam became the meeting place for black religious and political leadership from Georgia, South Carolina, and other states throughout the South. Pictured here in 1918 is the second pastor of Sardis Baptist Church, W.T. Johnson, assisted by Deacon Talley and Deacon Bostic in performing baptismal rites on Mother Willie Lewis, and her brother, Burrel Bryant, in 1918. (Courtesy of Juanita Byrd and Powerpointe Archives.)

The Kennesaw Association was set up by Sardis Baptist Church for the purpose of fellowship and to ensure that the Black Baptist churches were unified in their teachings and interpretation of the Bible. Traditionally, Baptist churches, unlike the AME churches, which had presiding elders and bishops to oversee the teachings and operations of all churches in its denomination, were not under any uniform body. Each church was left to its own policies and biblical interpretations. Pictured here is the Singing Convention of the Kennesaw Association *c.* 1945. (Courtesy of Juanita Byrd and Powerpointe Archives.)

Mt. Zion AME Church in Kennesaw has an oral history that dates back to the early 1830s. Church history recalls white settlers moving into Cobb County with their belongings to claim land given to them by the Georgia lotteries. The slaves of some of the white settlers from South Carolina are given credit for starting Mt. Zion AME Church. It is believed that these slaves had been exposed to Rev. Morris Brown of the AME Church in Charleston, South Carolina. Bishop Henry McNeal Turner became the first pastor of Mt. Zion AME Church between 1865 and 1866. In 1867, Turner brought the church into its first African Methodist Episcopal Conference. Mt. Zion AME Church is located on Wade Green Road in Kennesaw. Church records indicate the church has been in this same location since the 1860s. Presently, work is in progress to have both the church and cemetery listed on the National Registry of Historic Sites. (Courtesy of Powerpointe Archives.)

Historic Mt. Zion AME Cemetery sits in back of the church. The oldest legible marker is that of Isom Gresham, a former slave and rumored offspring of the white Gresham family. Born in 1809, Isom Gresham enjoyed privileges as a landowner and businessman. Church records indicate that Isom Gresham donated one acre of land to Mt. Zion AME Church before 1855. The earliest recorded death at Mt. Zion AME Cemetery was on September 26, 1855. Before 1838, the members of Mt. Zion buried their dead with their Cherokee neighbors in Franklin Cemetery, now known as Chastain Road. Later, Gresham and Chalker Cemeteries were used to bury the church's members. The use of Chalker Cemetery by the black church prompted Mr. Chalker, a white landowner and businessman, to donate two acres of land to be used as a cemetery for the black church's own use. (Courtesy of Powerpointe Archives.)

Turner Chapel AME Church is believed to be the second-oldest AME congregation in Georgia. The original site was located in the heart of downtown Marietta and was originally owned by the First Presbyterian Church of Marietta. In 1854, the church was purchased by freedmen and slaves, and was called Trinity Church for Negroes and Indians. During that time, they operated under the direction of the First Methodist Church. In 1865, Bishop Henry McNeal Turner came to Georgia and found ex-slaves and freedmen worshipping without a minister. He became the first black minister of the church. In 1891, under the leadership of Rev. Dan Strickland, the church was rebuilt and the name was changed to Turner Chapel AME in honor of Bishop Henry McNeal Turner. The old Turner Chapel AME Church is pictured here in the 1950s. (Courtesy of the Georgia Department of Archives and History.)

The congregation of Union Chapel United Methodist Church, Marietta, which was organized in the late 1880s, is shown here c. 1940. (Courtesy of John Patterson.)

Four

EDUCATION

From Church Schools To Public Schools

The old Noonday Church Schoolhouse for black children, seen here in 1900, is located in Kennesaw. Prior to the 1890s, there were no public schools in Marietta and Kennesaw. White students received their education in private schools held in private homes. Later, the academies and seminaries became the primary schools for white children, while black children depended on their community churches to provide them with a basic elementary education. In Kennesaw, the church schools for black children were Mt. Zion AME, Noonday Baptist, Liberty Baptist, Kennesaw, and Slocumb Hall. Later these church schools became a part of Cobb County's segregated public school system. (Courtesy of Powerpointe Archives.)

Hattie Lee Jackson Crawford Floyd (a Jackson descendant and the author's great-great-Aunt) was one of the pioneer elementary educators at Mt. Zion AME Church School in Kennesaw. She eventually became the superintendent of the school. After 1929, black children in Kennesaw could travel to Marietta to the only black high school in the area, Marietta Industrial High School, renamed Perkinson High and later renamed Lemon Street High School. (Courtesy of Hattie Floyd's daughter, Lula M. Michael, and grandson, Mike Clark.)

Marietta opened its first black public elementary school in 1894. Black children could attend the new elementary school from first through seventh grade. Referred to as "the colored school," Lemon Street Elementary started out, unlike the white public school, with no lights, inadequate furniture, and without books or supplies. The black principals and teachers received a substantially lower pay rate than did their white counterparts. Segregation laws in the South kept schools for black children inferior and substandard.

Pictured here in Marietta, c. 1951, is a Lemon Street Elementary classroom. (Courtesy of Hardy Studio, Marietta, Georgia.)

Pictured here is the Lemon Street Elementary class of 1924. (Courtesy of John Patterson and Powerpointe Archives.)

This unidentified black Elementary School in Kennesaw, *c.* 1930, stayed in use until the 1950s. (Courtesy of the Georgia Department of Archives and History.)

Pictured here is the Lemon Street seventh grade graduating class of 1918, with Professor C.L. Maxey (seated, second row, center), the school's third principal. Professor A. Tolliver was the school's first principal followed by Professor Luke B. Norris. Some of the earlier teachers at Lemon Street Elementary were Louella Woodward Patterson, who taught first grade in 1908 (Clark College graduate); J. Lena Sorrell, who taught third grade in 1912; W. Louis Henry, who taught seventh grade in 1919 (Spelman College graduate); Mamie F. Palmer, who taught first grade in 1916 (Morris Brown graduate); Marie Adams, who taught second grade in 1902; and Mamie Lou Fair, who taught third grade in 1903. (Courtesy of Powerpointe Archives.)

Marietta

PUBLIC SCHOOLS

RECORD OF GRADES

6th + 7th

Colored School BUILDING

FOR THE YEAR *1916 – 1917*

C. L. Maxey TEACHER

DIRECTIONS

1. Keep record for first few days on legal cap. By end of second week enter names in register, alphabetically, by grades

2. Make all entries in black ink, except the totals and averages at the close of year, which make in red ink.

3. Take age of pupils (who enroll the first half of year) at last birthday, unless the birthday comes before January 1st, in which case take age at next birthday. Take age at last birthday of all pupils who enter after January 1st.

4. When a pupil enters (after first half day), place a small x in the proper space. Indicate absence by a light mark (⁄) in the proper space.

5. When a pupil is absent more than six consecutive half days, enter a D (dropped) in place of the seventh mark.

6. When a pupil is tardy enter the number of minutes in the space corresponding to the half day in which the tardiness occurred.

7. In the lower right hand corner of space for name place B if a boy, G if a girl.

8. When a pupil is transferred to (T) another building or grade, or transferred from (TT) another building or grade, or has moved from the city, or has left school for cause, indicate the fact under Remarks on right hand page

9. Satisfactory excuse for absence must be brought from parents at the next session pupil attends school after absence If the excuse is accepted cancel the absent mark thus X.

10. When a pupil is transferred to (T), or transferred from (TT) a building or grade, the appropriate letter or letters must be entered in the space corresponding to the half day in which the change occurred, and a note made under Remarks.

11. When a pupil re-enters after having been dropped, place R in the proper space. The number of days a pupil is not enrolled in any month will be equal to one-half the blank spaces intervening between D and R, plus 1.

12. Make all entries with great care, and keep the record clean and neat.

13. Enter the name of every visitor on the last page of the record.

C.L. Maxey signs off on the 'Record of Grades' for his sixth and seventh grade classes in 1907. (Courtesy of Marietta City Schools.)

In 1953, an unidentified black elementary class in Cobb County wear their coats inside, indicating the unsatisfactory heating conditions in the classroom. The substandard conditions for black students in the South did not begin to change until after the U.S. Supreme Court outlawed racial segregation in public schools in the landmark case *Brown versus the Board of Education* in 1954. (Courtesy of the Georgia Department of Archives and History.)

Vallie B. Jackson (a Jackson descendant and the author's cousin) taught at Lemon Street Elementary in the early 1900s. A graduate of Spelman College, she devoted most of her time to the development of black children. Her 'Programme of Daily Work,' written in 1905, outlines what a typical day was like for her students. (Courtesy of Marietta City Schools.)

Programme of Daily Work

Time	A	B	C
9:00 – 9:15	Devotion — Roll Call		
9:15 – 9:30	Study nos.	Study nos.	Recite nos.
9:30 – 9:45	Study nos.	Recite nos.	Study Reading
9:45 – 10:05	Recite nos.	Study Reading	Board Work
10:05 – 10:25	Study Reading	Board Work	Recite Reading
10:25 – 10:35	Board Work	Recite Reading	Busy Work
10:35 – 10:45	Recite Reading	Busy Work	Study Spelling
10:45 – 11:00	Recess		
11:00 – 11:10	Chart Lesson		
11:10 – 11:20	Busy Work	Study Spelling	Recite Spelling
11:20 – 11:35	Copy sentences	Recite Spelling	Copy sentences
11:35 – 11:45	Calisthenics		
11:45 – 12:00	Study Spelling	Study Lang.	Recite Language
12:00 – 12:15	Recite Spelling	Copy sentences	Busy Work
12:15 – 12:30	Busy Work	Recite Lang.	Busy Work
12:30 – 12:45	Mon. + Wed. Drawing — Tues. Thurs. Friday Writing		
12:45 – 1:00	Recess		
1:00 – 1:10	Music		
1:10 – 1:25	Study Reading	Study Reading	Recite Reading
1:25 – 1:35	Recite Reading	Busy Work	Busy Work
1:35 – 1:50	Busy Work	Recite Reading	Busy Work
1:50 – 1:55	Boys Dismissed		
2:00	Girls Dismissed		

C 1905 1906   Vallie B. Jackson

43

Marietta Industrial High School was the first black high school in Marietta. Prior to this, the only secondary school in Marietta for black children was a single-room abandoned church on Harold Street. Marietta Industrial High School was the result of a joint effort spearheaded by the leadership of Mattie J. Durham, Ursula Maxwell Jenkins, and the black community. Additional "monies" were given by the Julius Rosenwald Fund, a program that made funds available for the construction of "adequate school buildings" for black children in Georgia. Marietta Industrial High School was completed in 1929. It was renamed Perkison High, and, in later years, the name was changed to Lemon Street High School. (Courtesy of John Patterson.)

Marietta's Harold Street School was the only secondary school for black children before the opening of Marietta Industrial High School—later known as Lemon Street High School. (Courtesy of Marietta City Schools.)

Ursula Maxwell Jenkins, seen here in the 1930s, was the first black teacher in what was known as the beginning of a secondary school for black children in Marietta, Harold Street School. After finishing high school at Spelman College, Jenkins stayed on until she completed her college education in 1903. Ursula Maxwell worked with Mattie J. Durham to raise funding for the first black high school in Marietta.

Louella Woodward Patterson (far right) is pictured here in the 1940s with her first grade class. She taught at Lemon Street Elementary for more than 30 years. Finishing as the valedictorian of her Lemon Street Elementary class in 1898, Mrs. Patterson went on to pursue her high school and college education at Clark College in Atlanta. After retiring in 1952 at the age of 70, she continued her work with children at the Cole Street Nursery in Marietta. (Courtesy of John Patterson.)

Ms. Louella Woodward Patterson (center) graduated from Clark College in 1904. (John Patterson.)

Marion J. Woods, seen here c. 1937, was the principal of Marietta school system's first black high school. He also coached the football team, drove the school bus, and made repairs around the school. He was an active member of Zion Baptist Church. (Courtesy of Marietta City Schools.)

Leanna Tanner Wilcox, a Kennesaw native, taught in the school systems of Cobb County, Cherokee County, and in the state of South Carolina for more than 40 years. Leanna is pictured here with one of her English and math classes, c. 1925. (Courtesy of Juanita Byrd.)

Leanna Tanner Wilcox is pictured here, c. 1925, with her elementary class. (Courtesy of Juanita Byrd.)

Five

WORKING FOR US

The ending of slavery in 1865 gave black men, women, and children the opportunity to become wage earners. Southern blacks were now able to work towards building strong families and communities. Pictured here in 1900 are cotton pickers in Marietta. (Courtesy of Hardy Studio, Marietta, Georgia.)

From the 1880s through the turn of the century, census records reflect a steady increase in the numbers of blacks migrating into Kennesaw and Marietta. Black men sought jobs as part of the extra-gang and section-gang crews on the Western & Atlantic Railway. These men were instrumental in the construction and maintenance of the railroad.

In the town area of Marietta, Brumby Chair Company, McNeel Marble Co., and Glover Machine Works were some of the businesses that offered employment to black workers. Toward the end of the century, tax digest records indicate that Marietta was one of the few districts in Cobb County that had a large percentage of its black population listed as landowners. The 1880 census lists some of the occupations held by black workers in Marietta as laborer, barber, seamstress, washwoman, chambermaid, and "keeping house."

Kennesaw, unlike the town of Marietta, still remained agriculturally driven with cotton and Indian corn being their primary crops. Census records in the Big Shanty area of Kennesaw list black workers as farm laborers and farmers. After 1900, Kennesaw began to see a marginal increase in the number of black farmers who owned their land. The 1909 Tax Digests for Cobb County, the Big Shanty area, show 721 acres of land owned by blacks. This farmland now makes up parts of Chastain Road, Big Shanty Road, Kennesaw State College, Vulcan Materials Company, and other developed areas of Kennesaw.

Some of the black farm-owners listed in Big Shanty in 1909 were Deacon Sam Bostick owning 40 acres, Hamp Jackson owning 66 acres, John Jackson (son of Hamp Jackson) owning 30 acres, and Alfred Lowe owning 120 acres.

The occupation of nurse midwifery was dominated by black women during much of the 20th century. In Kennesaw and Marietta, black and white births were presided over by the nurse midwives, as was also the case for much of the rural South. These women would attend to the sick, prescribe herbs and roots for common illnesses, and help in the preparation of bodies for funerals. The most remembered nurse midwife was Mrs. Lucille Tanner McAfee, who delivered more than 400 babies over the span of her career.

During the 1920s through the 1940s, the number of black businesses increased in Marietta. The first black taxi-cab service was started by businessman A.S. "Shine" Fowler. Hanley Company Funeral Directors became the first black funeral home started in 1928 by J.H. Hanley. Prominent businessman and outspoken Republican Andrew Rogers owned a barbershop, ice cream parlor, and dance hall in the downtown area of Marietta during the early 1920s.

Mr. Summerour, c. 1900, was among a growing number of black men who owned and farmed their land. He owned land in Powder Springs and Kennesaw. (Courtesy of Powerpointe Archives.)

McNeal Marble Company's first plant was brought from the McClatchey Brothers in 1892. This plant specialized in the construction of cemetery and Civil War monuments and statues. Four unidentified black men, seen here around 1892, made up a part of the work crew of the first plant, which is still located at its original location on Whitlock Avenue in Marietta. (Courtesy of the Georgia Department of Archives.)

The McNeal Marble Company's second plant worked on cemetery monuments, Civil War statues, and World War I and World War II monuments. Eleven unidentified black workers, seen here c. 1896, made up a part of the work crew. (Courtesy of the Georgia Department of Archives and History.)

Black and white workers, in the foreground of this photograph dating from 1890 and taken in Cobb County, were hired by the Western & Atlantic Railroad to work as part of the section gang crews. Their responsibilities included re-grading and laying railroad tracks. (Courtesy of the Georgia Department of Archives and History.)

Emma Tanner (center) with daughter Angeline Tanner (first from left) and two unidentified women are pictured here, c. 1900, in Kennesaw de-weeding cotton on their land. Emma Tanner was the wife of Deacon A.J. Tanner, farm owner and one of the founding fathers of Sardis Baptist Church, started in 1880. (Courtesy of Juanita Byrd and Powerpointe Archives.)

Crescent Pressing Club was located on Root Street at the square of Marietta. Three unidentified black workers are shown here around 1904. (Courtesy of the Georgia Department of Archives and History.)

This picture, c. 1917, is believed to be of Arthur Jones laying the first brick and marking the beginning of paved roads in Marietta. (Courtesy of the Georgia Department of Archives and History.)

The Glover Machine Work Shop Crew is seen here around 1920. Black men worked for Glover Machine Works, located on Butler Street in Marietta, as part of the machine shop and foundry crews which handled locomotive construction. (Courtesy of the Georgia Department of Archives and History.)

Pictured around 1890 in Marietta is an unidentified black man making syrup. (Courtesy of the Marietta Museum of History.)

Seen here, c. 1890, is an unidentified child sitting on corn in front of a tool shed used by black tenant farmers between Marietta and Kennesaw. (Courtesy of the Georgia Department of Archives and History.)

A prominent black businessman and outspoken Republican, Andrew Rogers owned a barber shop, ice cream parlor, and dance hall in the building located next to the Marietta courthouse. In this picture, dating from around 1920, the courthouse is the building on the far right with the clock on top. (Courtesy of the Georgia Department of Archives and History.)

Roy Gober, *c.* 1916, stands in front of the Cole family home. He began working for the Coles at the age of 12 while attending school at Lemon Street. (Courtesy of the Georgia Department of Archives and History.)

Pictured here is an unidentified black man and child on a wagon at Ruff's Mill in Marietta, *c.* 1900. (Courtesy of Marietta City Schools.)

Lucille Tanner McAfee, a Marietta resident, was born in Kennesaw in the 1890s and is seen here around 1920. She delivered more than 400 babies during her career as a nurse midwife. (Courtesy of Juanita Byrd and Powerpointe Archives.)

Pictured here is Clara Blackwell, c. 1890. She worked as a nurse and nurse midwife in Marietta. (Courtesy of the Georgia Department of Archives and History.)

The late businessman, A.S. "Shine" Fowler (the author's cousin), was known by the black people in Marietta as "The Mayor of Lawrence Street" because of his many businesses on that street in the late 1930s. A successful entrepreneur, he owned a restaurant, the first black taxi-cab service in Marietta, and numerous properties. This photograph of Mr. Fowler dates from the 1930s. (Courtesy of Ruby Haley and Powerpointe Archives.)

This advertisement is for Hanley Company, who, in 1928, was the fifth funeral home to open in Cobb County while becoming the first black-owned funeral home in Marietta. Started by owner J.H. Hanley, the business was later sold by D.H. Holmes to H.E. Shelton in 1985 and the name was changed to Hanley-Shelton Funeral Home. Still located in Marietta, Hanley-Shelton Funeral Home continues to service the black communities of Marietta, Kennesaw, and other surrounding cities.

HANLEY COMPANY

FUNERAL DIRECTORS

We Carry a Complete Line of
Funeral Necessities
Open Day and Night

Private Ambulance Service
Our Prices Are the Lowest
No Deserving Poor Refused
120 Lawrence St.   Phone 657
Marietta, Ga.
J. H. Hanley, Preesident
D. H. Holmes, Manager
Mrs. L. A. Davison, Sec'y-Treas.

Pictured here on Lawrence Street in Marietta is the old building of Hanley Company Funeral Parlor, which was located on the left side of the building. Shine Fowler's restaurant and taxi-cab service was on the right side of the building. Upstairs (middle door entrance) is where the black Masonic Lodge was located c. 1959. (Courtesy of the Georgia Department of Archives and History.)

This is the original building of Bradley Eppinger and Sons Funeral Home in Marietta. Bradley Eppinger and Sons was the eighth funeral home to open in Cobb County as a corporation. The owners included Barrington McCarter "Shine," Bradley Eppinger Sr., A.S. Fowler, J.Q. Caruthers, and George McKenny. (Courtesy of Bridgette Eppinger Greene.)

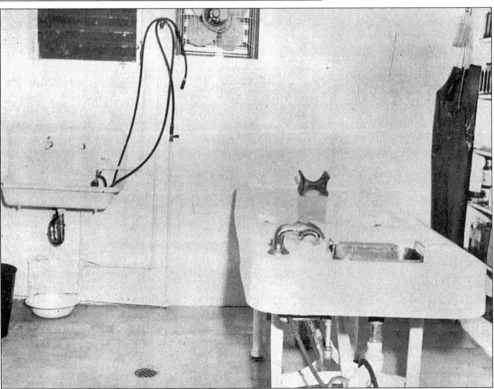

The operating room of Bradley Eppinger and Sons Funeral Home is seen here in around 1950. (Courtesy of Bridgette Eppinger Greene.)

Bradley Eppinger and Sons Funeral Home was located at 30 Holliday Street, Marietta. It is seen here in around 1950 at their second location. In 1952, Mr. and Mrs. Bradley E. Eppinger became sole proprietors and changed the name to Marietta Funeral Parlor. Years later, the name was changed to Mack Eppinger & Sons Funeral Services, which is presently located on North Barrow Street in Cartersville, Georgia. The granddaughter of Mr. and Mrs. Eppinger, Bridgette Eppinger Greene, currently manages all operations at the funeral home. (Courtesy of Bridgette Eppinger Greene.)

Pictured here are Mack Eppinger and Bradley Eppinger Sr.

Pictured here in around 1960 is Bradley Eppinger Sr. (standing, center) with his family. (Courtesy of Bridgette Eppinger Greene.)

Mrs. Mabel Eppinger, wife of Bradley Eppinger Sr., is remembered as the business mind behind Mack Eppinger and Sons Funeral Parlor. (Courtesy of Bridgette Eppinger Greene.)

Ruby Haley, seen here c. 1950, opened her Beauty, Barber and Cosmetic Shop in the late 1940s. Lawrence Street in Marietta was the location where black-owned businesses thrived during the 1920s through the 1950s. (Courtesy of Ruby Haley.)

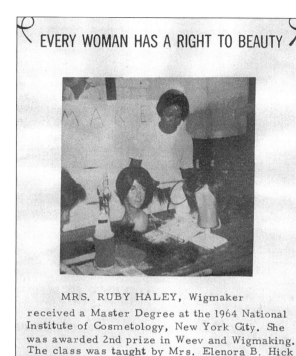

EVERY WOMAN HAS A RIGHT TO BEAUTY

MRS. RUBY HALEY, Wigmaker received a Master Degree at the 1964 National Institute of Cosmetology, New York City. She was awarded 2nd prize in Weev and Wigmaking. The class was taught by Mrs. Elenora B. Hick M. C. of Richmond, Virginia.

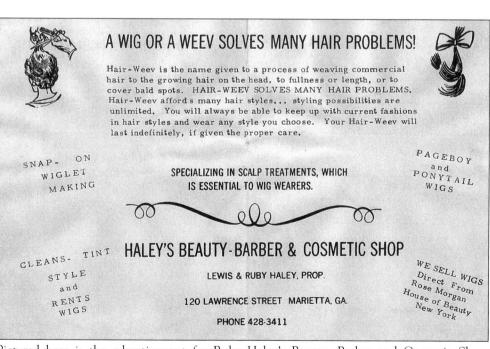

A WIG OR A WEEV SOLVES MANY HAIR PROBLEMS!

Hair-Weev is the name given to a process of weaving commercial hair to the growing hair on the head, to fullness or length, or to cover bald spots. HAIR-WEEV SOLVES MANY HAIR PROBLEMS. Hair-Weev affords many hair styles... styling possibilities are unlimited. You will always be able to keep up with current fashions in hair styles and wear any style you choose. Your Hair-Weev will last indefinitely, if given the proper care.

SNAP-ON WIGLET MAKING

SPECIALIZING IN SCALP TREATMENTS, WHICH IS ESSENTIAL TO WIG WEARERS.

PAGEBOY and PONYTAIL WIGS

CLEANS-TINT STYLE and RENTS WIGS

HALEY'S BEAUTY-BARBER & COSMETIC SHOP

LEWIS & RUBY HALEY, PROP.

120 LAWRENCE STREET MARIETTA, GA.

PHONE 428-3411

WE SELL WIGS Direct From Rose Morgan House of Beauty New York

Pictured here is the advertisement for Ruby Haley's Beauty, Barber and Cosmetic Shop. Ruby Haley leased office space from businessman "Shine" Fowler to open her shop. (Courtesy of Ruby Haley.)

R.L. Summerour of Kennesaw (second row, fifth from left) is seen here working at the Lockheed Plant in Marietta during the 1940s. Lockheed, founded in 1913 as an aircraft company, later expanded into the aerospace industry, excelling in aviation, missiles, space platforms, and satellites. Lockheed, more than any single commercial corporation had the responsibilities for key offensive and defensive weapons systems of the Cold War. (Courtesy of Mary Summerour.)

Six
THE DOBBS FAMILY

Grand Lodge Officers 1920

1. J. H. WALKER, D. G. M.
2. H. R. BUTLER, M. W. G. M.
3. J. W. DOBBS, G. S W.

4. W. D. SAVAGE, G. J. W.
5. SOL. C. JOHNSON, G. S.
6. G. L. BOWEN, G. T.

John Wesley Dobbs, Grand Lodge Officer (#3), is pictured here in this rare photograph celebrating the golden anniversary of the Grand Lodge of Prince Hall Masons of Georgia c. 1920. (Courtesy of Juliet Dobbs Blackburn-Beamon, DA.)

One noted family with beginnings in Kennesaw is the Dobbs family of Atlanta. Most Atlantans are familiar with some of the descendants who are living now.

Maynard Holbrook Jackson Jr., elected the first black mayor of Atlanta in 1973, and Mattiwilda "Greekie" Dobbs Janzon, noted international opera singer, are among these descendants.

The patriarch through whom all these descendants are connected was John Wesley Dobbs. Born in Kennesaw in 1882, John Wesley lived the first part of his childhood with grandparents, uncles, and extended family. Later, he moved to Savannah with his mother and sister.

John Wesley Dobbs moved to Atlanta around 1897 where he enrolled at the Academy of the Atlanta Baptist College. This school would later become Morehouse College. Having to leave the academy due to the sickness of his mother, John Wesley obtained a job as a railway mail clerk. He later co-founded and led the Atlanta Negro Voters League, became one of the original directors of the first black bank, Citizens Trust Bank, became "Grand Master" of the Prince Hall Masons, was an outspoken political advocate for racial fairness and equality, an eloquent orator, and a staunch supporter of the NAACP. He was responsible for naming Auburn Avenue "Sweet Auburn," the name commonly referred to by people today.

John Wesley Dobbs credited a large part of his success to his early life in Kennesaw. His experiences with his grandparents and uncles were told to his children and grandchildren throughout the years. A strong sense of family was one of his most admirable characteristics, and this was largely due to the love he received as a child from his Kennesaw family. He frequently spoke of his close relationship with his uncle Jesse, who was like a brother to him.

John Wesley Dobbs died in Atlanta on August 30, 1961, on the day that nine black students began the integration of the city's public schools.

Wesley and Judie Dobbs, grandparents of John Wesley Dobbs, are shown here on this 1870 census. Wesley Dobbs worked very hard as a farm laborer and was able to support his family despite the unfair and inequitable wages that were paid to most of the newly emancipated blacks.

Judie Dobbs is remembered by her family as a "Proud Lady." She lived to be more than 90 years old. The mother of 14 children, Judie and her husband Wesley are remembered as always sharing what little they had with family and friends. This picture dates from around 1900. (Courtesy of Juliet Dobbs Blackburn-Beamon, DA.)

Minnie Hendricks Dobbs Banks (who may have also been related to the McAfees in this area) is seen here around 1900. She was born in Woodstock, Georgia, in 1862 and was the mother of John Wesley Dobbs. She married Will Dobbs of Kennesaw, and they had two children. John Wesley Dobbs gave his mother credit for pushing him and his sister Willie to be the best they could be. Minnie is remembered by her family as being a "sharp" dresser, especially in preparation for Sunday morning at Noonday Baptist Church services. (Courtesy of Juliet Dobbs Blackburn-Beamon, DA.)

John Wesley Dobbs is pictured here, *c.* 1892, with his only sibling, Willie Dobbs. (Juliet Dobbs Blackburn-Beamon, DA.)

Jesse Dobbs was commonly known as the brother of John Wesley Dobbs but he was actually his uncle. Only eight years older than John Wesley, Jesse Dobbs remained his close friend and "brother" throughout his life. John convinced his Uncle Jesse to move his family to Atlanta in 1920. He helped his Uncle Jesse secure a job as a janitor at the black branch of the Carnegie Library. Jesse Dobbs and his family would return to Kennesaw every summer to work the farm and visit with relatives. Jesse, the former Sunday School superintendent of Sardis Baptist, would spearhead the annual picnics for the church, usually held at the black country club resort Kings Wigwam. (Courtesy of Dr. Blanche Dobbs.)

Lizzie Bedford Dobbs, seen here around 1890, was the wife of Jesse Dobbs. (Courtesy of Dr. Blanche Dobbs.)

Sardis Bapt. S. S.
Kennesaw, Ga. Mar. 15 – 190

Sardis sunday school assemble in Sardis Ch
at the usual hour for sunday school.
The supt. read the 1st. Psalm, and asked Go
blessings upon us.
Singing.
          The lesson was nicely taught us by Bo.
Florence,
(Jesus heals a man born blind, John 9th.
(I am the light of the world, John 9:5, golden te.
The weather was fine.
The attendants were good.
Several visitors were with us.
Some very good thing were said to us, b
Rev. T. M. Allen, and W. M. Strickling
Singing, no. 21: what a friend,
Collection 28 ℓ.
              Dismissed by Rev. W. M. Strickling,
                  J. L. Dobbs, Supt.
                    G. L. Dobbs, sec.

Sardis Baptist Church records of the Sunday school class held on March 15, 1908, are shown here. J.L. (Jesse) Dobbs was acting superintendent and his brother G.L (George) Dobbs was the secretary. (Courtesy of Juanita Byrd.)

72

Jesse Dobbs, like John Wesley Dobbs, believed in the tradition of family, which remained a very important part of his life. The children of Jesse Dobbs are pictured here, *c.* 1950. They are, from left to right, Guy (oldest), Robert Lee, Jesse Sr., Isabel Dobbs Gassette (seated), Jesse Jr., and Wesley (youngest). (Courtesy of Dr. Blanche Dobbs.)

John Wesley Dobbs's love of family is shown here in this 1952 Dobbs family reunion photograph. The future first black mayor of Atlanta, Maynard H. Jackson is pictured in the back row, second from the left. (Courtesy of Juliet Dobbs Blackburn-Beamon, DA.)

Seven
THE JACKSON FAMILY
Finding My Roots

Sandal Jackson, a widow, and her family settled in Kennesaw and Marietta in the 1870s. She was married to Alex N. Jackson, who died in 1855 in Upson County, Georgia. Alex and Sandal Jackson had 11 children. Sandal's father was a full-blooded Cherokee and her mother was believed to have been part African and part Cherokee. Little is known about Alexander except that he was also of Cherokee ancestry. The author is the great-great-great-granddaughter of Sandal and Alex Jackson, the great-great-granddaughter of Hamp and Louisa Johnson Jackson, the great-granddaughter of Robert Alexander and Capitola Fowler Jackson, and the granddaughter of Benjamin and Jennie Louise Jackson Hall. Many descendants of Sandal and Alex can be found in Kennesaw, Marietta, and the surrounding Atlanta metropolitan area today. Jackson ancestors were literate, educated their children, owned land, voted, and owned stock during the turn of the century. Many of the older people in Kennesaw and Marietta still talk about the children of Sandal and Alex Jackson almost 120 years later.

Note A.—The Census Year begins June 1, 1879, and ends May 31, 1880.

Note B.—All persons will be included in the Enumeration who were living on the 1st day of June, 1880. ... June 1, 1880, will be OMITTED. Members of Families who have DIED SINCE June 1, 1880, w...

Note C.—Questions Nos. 13, 14, 22 and 23 are not to be asked in respect to persons under 10 years of age.

1.—Inhabitants in _Marietta_, in the County of _Cobb_, enumerated by me on the _6th_ day of June, 1880.

Sandal Jackson, the author's great-great-great-grandmother, was the first known generation of the Jackson family to have lived in Marietta or Kennesaw. Census records place Sandal Jackson and her family in Kennesaw and Marietta around the 1870s. Sandal was born in 1819 in Virginia and died in Marietta in 1897. She had 11 children of which 8 were living in 1906. This 1880 census shows Sandal living with her daughter Rhody, granddaughter Emma, and son-in-law John Braxton. The census taker listed their race as mulatto.

Hampton (Hamp) and Louisa (Lula) Jackson (author's great-great-grandparents) stand in front of the old family home on what is now known as Duncan Road in Kennesaw, c. 1910. The second generation of the Jackson family in Marietta and Kennesaw was Hamp Jackson and nine of his siblings. Hamp was born in 1850 in Upson County, Georgia, and was the second son of Sandal and Alex Jackson. Hamp married Louisa Johnson, and they had 14 children of whom 10 were living in 1906. Lula was a teacher and a nurse. Hamp Jackson was a respected member and steward at Mt. Zion AME Church in Kennesaw. He purchased 66 1/3 acres of land in 1907 and farmed the land for 25 years until his death in 1932. His land made up parts of Kennesaw State College, Vulcan Quarry, and other developed areas of Kennesaw today. (Courtesy of Jimmy Roberts and Powerpointe Archives.)

This picture of deed shows that Hamp Jackson purchased land in 1907. Hamp Jackson is remembered as a smart businessman. The 1910 census taker for Big Shanty in Cobb County, Edward G. Carrie, lists Hamp Jackson and his entire family as literate. Before 1900, census records classify Hamp Jackson as a mulatto. After 1900, his classification became black. (Courtesy of Cobb County Deed Office.)

Lizzie Winters Northcutt, noted philanthropist, sold Hamp Jackson 106 acres in Kennesaw in 1907 for $600. Forty acres of the land was given to Janie McGee, Hamp Jackson's sister-in-law. (Courtesy of Linda Northcutt.)

STERN CHEROKEES.

APPLICATION

OF

...pton Jackson

...te of money appropriated for the Eastern Cherokee
by the Act of Congress approved June 30, 1906, in
...ce with the decrees of the Court of Claims of May
, and May 28, 1906

No. 33930

No. 33930

Name

With No. 32125

Remarks:

Hampton Jackson

In 1906 Hamp Jackson and nine of his siblings residing in Kennesaw and Marietta applied to the Eastern Band of the Cherokees. In order to participate, the applicant had to be alive on May 28, 1906, and establish himself as a member of the Eastern Cherokee or a descendant of a member living at the time of the violated treaties. In 1906, Guion Miller was appointed by the U.S. Court of Claims to determine who was eligible for funds under the treaties of 1835–36 and 1845 between the United States and the Eastern Cherokee. In the ruling made by the Court of Claims of the United States decided on March 7, 1910, the court specifically excluded applicants who had disassociated themselves from the Cherokee tribe as well as those persons and descendants who had traced their Cherokee ancestry through an ancestor who was a slave or through an ancestor who was born a slave. It can be assumed that most black or mulatto applicants who had Cherokee ancestry were not accepted. Full-blooded Cherokee slaves and their offspring were also denied acceptance into the Eastern Band of the Cherokees. (Courtesy of National Archives.)

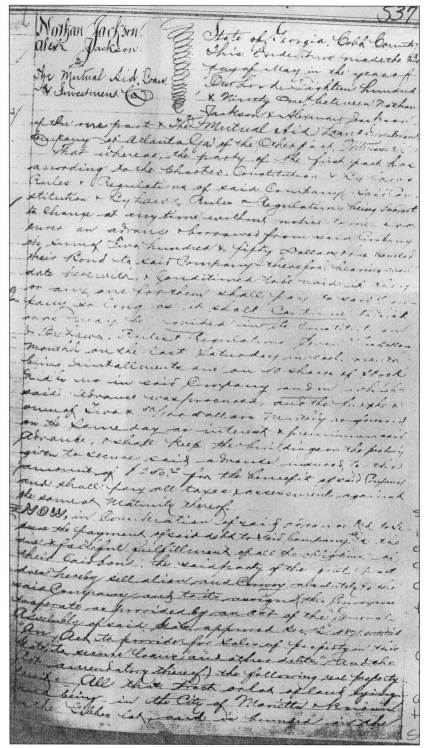

Nathan and Alex Jackson, brothers of Hamp Jackson, purchased stock in the Mutual Aid & Loan Investment Company, recorded in the Cobb County deed office, 1880.

Pictured here are Daisy Jackson Hall and her husband, Rev. J.H. Hall, a prominent minister and presiding elder of the AME Church. Daisy was the oldest daughter of Hamp and Lula Jackson and was born in Kennesaw in 1878. She was a schoolteacher in Rockmart, Georgia. (Courtesy of Johnson Family Archives.)

Willie Bell Hall-Johnson, seen here c. 1920, is the daughter of Rev. J.H. Hall and Daisy Jackson Hall. She was a graduate of Georgia State Industrial College, which later became Savannah State College. Willie Bell, age 90, currently lives in California. (Courtesy of Johnson Family Archives.)

Addie Jackson Roberts was the second daughter of Hamp and Louisa Jackson. Born in 1882, she married Willie Roberts and moved to Marietta where they lived for many years. Both she and her husband are buried in the old Mt. Zion AME Cemetery in Kennesaw. The grandson of Addie and Willie Roberts, Eugene Roberts lives in the Marietta area today. (Courtesy of Jimmy Roberts and Eugene Roberts, grandsons of Addie and Willie Roberts.)

Fermin Loren Jackson was the ninth child of Hamp and Louisa Jackson and was born in 1893 in Kennesaw. (Courtesy of Powerpointe Archives.)

Robert Alexander Jackson (author's great-grandfather) and his siblings are the third generation descendants of Sandal and Alex Jackson. Born on December 20, 1880, in Kennesaw, Robert Alexander Jackson was the second son of Hamp and Louisa (Lula) Jackson. He married Capitola "Cappie" Fowler in 1902. She was the daughter of Mr. and Mrs. Cicero Fowler and the first cousin of A.S. "Shine" Fowler. They had seven children including the author's grandmother, Jennie Louise Jackson Hall. Robert Alexander assisted his father in running the family farm for several years, later moving to Marietta where he worked for McNeal Marble Company until his death. He was a stone cutter who worked on tombstones and monuments. Both Robert Alexander and Capitola Fowler Jackson are buried at the back of Mt. Zion AME's century-and-a-half-old cemetery. (Courtesy of Powerpointe Archives.)

Recalled as a strong, loving mother and devoted church member, Capitola Fowler (author's great-grandmother) is fondly remembered as "Mother Cappie." She was left to raise all of her children after the early death of her husband, Robert Alexander, in 1921. (Courtesy of Powerpointe Archives.)

This is a picture of the marriage license of Robert Alexander and Cappie Fowler from 1902. (Courtesy of Cobb County Records.)

STATE OF GEORGIA. COBB COUNTY.

To any Minister of the Gospel, Judge of the Superior Court, or Justice of the Peace to Celebrate:

You are Hereby Authorized To join in the HONORABLE STATE OF

Robert Jackson p. o. c. and Cappie Fo

according to the Rules of your Church, provided there be no lawful cause to obstruct the same, or

the Constitution and Laws of this State; and for so doing this shall be your sufficient License.

Given under my hand and seal, this 17th day of March 1902.

John Austin

I Hereby Certify, That Robert Jackson

Cappie Fowler were joined together

HOLY BANS OF MATRIMONY,

on the 17th day of March 1902, by me.

A. Blossom same

85

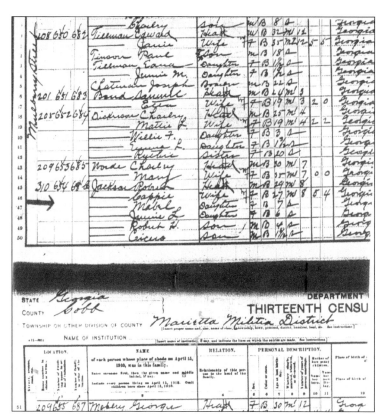

Mabel Jackson, shown on the census as living in Marietta Militia District, was the oldest daughter of Robert and Capitola Jackson. She died several years after this 1910 census was taken. (Courtesy of Decatur Library.)

Cicero Jackson, second son of Robert and Capitola Jackson, is shown here standing with his first wife on family land in Kennesaw c. 1920. Years later he remarried to Mrs. Katie Jackson and moved to Detroit, Michigan. They had three children. (Courtesy of Powerpointe Archives.)

Gertrude Jackson Booker was the third daughter of Robert and Capitola Fowler. She was born in Marietta in 1915 and lived there until her death in 1968. She married Mr. James C. Booker and they had two daughters, Harriet Booker Scott and Muriel Booker, who still reside in the old family home today. (Courtesy of Powerpointe Archives.)

Gilbert Jackson, a graduate of Morris Brown College and World War II veteran, was the third son of Robert and Capitola Jackson. Born in 1911, he married Ernestine Jackson, and they had three daughters. He lived in Marietta until his death in 1967. His wife lives in Marietta, and daughter Leslie Jackson Roscoe lives in metropolitan Atlanta. (Courtesy of Powerpointe Archives.)

This portrait of Gilbert Jackson's family dates from around 1940. The third child, Jennifer Jackson, is not shown here. This picture was taken before Gilbert's tour of duty in World War II.

Alexander Jackson, former World War II veteran, was the youngest son of Robert and Capitola Jackson. He married Reginia Jackson, and they had five children. Two of his children, JoAnn Jackson Martin and Alexander Jackson Jr., and their families, presently live in the Marietta area. (Courtesy of Powerpointe Archives.)

Robert H. Jackson, the oldest son of Robert and Capitola, was born in 1906. He married Georgia Jackson and lived in Marietta until his death. (Courtesy of Powerpointe Archives.)

Jennie Louise Jackson Hall, fourth generation descendant of Sandal and Alex Jackson and the author's grandmother, was born in 1904 in Marietta. She is pictured here, c. 1950, with her husband Benjamin F. Hall. They had three daughters—Venice Hall Lipsey, Capitola Hall Cooper, and the author's mother Ursula Hall Shelton. Jennie Louise was the second daughter of Robert Alexander and Capitola Jackson. She attended Lemon Street Elementary School in the early 1900s where she graduated with honors and later received her college education at Morris Brown College (AME Church School) in Atlanta. She devoted several years to teaching black students in the Bartow County school system in Cartersville, Georgia, before moving to North Carolina. (Courtesy of Powerpointe Archives.)

Jennie Louise Jackson married Benjamin F. Hall in 1928 and moved to Statesville, North Carolina. Her husband was the first black man to work and supervise at the Coca-Cola bottling plant in Statesville, North Carolina. Pictured here, *c.* 1929, is Benjamin F. Hall (standing, first, left) with his drivers at the Coca-Cola plant in Statesville, North Carolina. (Courtesy of Powerpointe Archives.)

Jennie Louise Jackson Hall (standing, third from left) continued in her family's tradition as a member of the AME denomination. She is seen here posing with the Center Street AME Zion Church Choir in Statesville, North Carolina. Jennie taught in the North Carolina and Pennsylvania school systems. (Courtesy of Powerpointe Archives.)

The mother of five children (two from a previous marriage), Jennie Louise Jackson later taught in the school systems in Statesville, North Carolina, and in York, Pennsylvania. In 1970, she and her husband moved to Decatur, Georgia, where they both lived until their respective deaths in 1974 and 1983. (Courtesy of Powerpointe Archives.)

The youngest daughter of Benjamin and Jennie Louise Jackson Hall, Ursula Hall Shelton (author's mother) moved to the Atlanta metropolitan area with her former husband, Waytus C. Shelton Sr., and their four children in the late 1960s. Her oldest son, Waytus C. Shelton Jr., and his family presently live in a subdivision in Kennesaw about a mile away from the 66 1/3 acres that his great-great-grandfather owned. Close by is the Mt. Zion AME Church and Cemetery, where many Jackson ancestors are buried. (Courtesy of Powerpointe Archives.)

Reginald Kemp, the great-great-grandson of Sandal and Alexander Jackson, lived most of his life in Marietta. He served in the United States Army in 1953 and served in the Korean War, receiving the Foreign Service Medal and the Korean National Medal. (Courtesy of Reginald Kemp.)

Pictured here is Edna Jackson Kemp, mother of Reginald Kemp and great-granddaughter of Sandal and Alexander Jackson. (Courtesy of Reginald Kemp.)

Reginald Kemp (back row, sixth from the left) is pictured in this rare Korean War photograph. (Courtesy of Reginald Kemp.)

Eight

PHOTOGRAPHER RAYMOND BUFORD

The Man with the Camera

"Mr. Raymond Buford would be coming up the street with his camera, wanting to take every body's [sic] picture. It got so, everyone knew what he wanted before he walked up to you."

—Mrs. Ernestine Jackson, Marietta

Raymond Buford is pictured here, c. 1940, in Marietta. Black folks in Atlanta had Paul Poole as a local photographer, while the blacks in Marietta had Raymond Buford. Although some of the black community would visit Paul Poole's studio in Atlanta on special occasions, the majority would call on photographer Raymond Buford to take pictures of their social clubs, children's recitals, and other important occasions. Mr. Buford is known to have taken pictures in Marietta from the late 1920s through the 1950s. Shortly after his death, Raymond Buford's negatives were thrown away, ending up on the city's garbage truck. He had no children or relatives to preserve his legacy. Fortunately, the Georgia Department of Archives and some of the black families in Marietta retained some of the later photographs taken by Mr. Raymond Buford, "the man with the camera." (Courtesy of Ruby Haley.)

Women's social clubs were popular in the 1930s and 1940s in most black communities in the South. Raymond Buford was frequently hired by social groups and organizations to take group pictures of the members. The Black Womens Social Club of Marietta is shown here, c. 1941. Members pictured here, from left to right, are as follows: (front row seated) Evelyn T. Gordon, Ernestine Henson Jackson (author's great-aunt), Ruby Bryant, Mary J. Allen Gullatt, Ruth Fraizer, and Lottie Mae Reed Devaughn; (back row standing) Elsie Stovall, Pearl McAfee Parnell, Gertrude Jackson Booker (author's great-aunt), and Emma Reedow. (Courtesy of Ernestine Jackson and Powerpointe Archives.)

Some of the black people in Marietta went to Paul Poole Studios, located in Atlanta at 151 and 3/4 Auburn Avenue. Pictured here in this Paul Poole original, c. 1920, is Gilbert Jackson (author's great-uncle), a graduate of Morris Brown College and one of the founders of the American Legion in Marietta. (Courtesy of Powerpointe Archives.)

Reuben Johnson (third from the left) worked with the Clay family for 65 years. This picture was taken on Montgomery Street in Marietta in front of the Clay home, c. 1947. (Powerpointe Archives.)

This family portrait of husband and wife, Willie and Addie Jackson Roberts (author's great-great-aunt), dates from around 1948. (Courtesy of Jimmy Roberts.)

Marietta had one of the first black Little League teams in Cobb County. This picture of the team was taken by Mr. Raymond Buford in 1954. (Courtesy of Powerpointe Archives.)

Jennifer Jackson poses for photographer Raymond Buford, c. 1950s. (Courtesy of Ernestine Jackson.)

Sandra Jackson and date (unidentified) pose for her first prom picture taken by Mr. Raymond Buford c. 1953. (Courtesy of Ernestine Jackson.)

This picture shows the piano recital of Sandra Jackson, which was held at Lyman Hall in Marietta, c. 1955. Most black socials and recreational events were held at Lyman Hall. (Courtesy of Ernestine Jackson.)

Nine

IMAGES

An unidentified woman is pictured in Marietta, *c.* 1880. Many of the photographs in this chapter were collected from various black families in Marietta and Kennesaw. Some of their stories have been remembered by family and friends, while others have simply faded away with each passing generation. The images tell us something about the lives and times of the people, forever captured in these photographs. (Courtesy of John Patterson and Powerpointe Archives.)

Marietta's "Tisha Mingoes Band" played at some of the social events for both the black and white communities. They are remembered for their performances at the Masonic Hall and the grand opening of the Marietta Country Club in 1915. Pictured here, c. 1915, the band consists of Theodore Ulysses Patterson (drums), Haywood Clark (violin), Essie Clark (piano), Mr. George Brook (trombone), and Arbe Gresham (trumpet). (Courtesy of John Patterson and Powerpointe Archives.)

The children of Theodore U. Patterson and Louella Woodward of Marietta are seen here, c. 1915. They are, from left to right, John Patterson and Jean Patterson. (Courtesy of John Patterson and Powerpointe Archives.)

Otho Jackson Woodward's family moved to Marietta around the late 1860s. He was a Buffalo Soldier with the Tenth Cavalry of the Union Army and later fought in the Spanish-American War. This picture of Otho dates from around 1863. (Courtesy of John Patterson and Powerpointe Archives.)

An unknown black couple are pictured here during the early 1900s. They are believed to be on Mulberry Street in Marietta. (Courtesy of Powerpointe Archives and Mr. John Patterson.)

Several unidentified men, both black and white, stand in front of the Marietta Freight Depot (foreground) and Marietta Paper Company. They are seen here observing a man with a bear on a leash, c. 1902. (Courtesy of the Georgia Department of Archives and History.)

Maggie Howard of Marietta is seen in this photograph holding peaches in each hand representing Georgia as the "Peach State." She sent relatives this picture of herself from Atlanta Baptist College in 1912. (Courtesy of Powerpointe Archives.)

G. A. R. Parade during Convention,
April, 1912, Marietta, Ga.

The annual Grand Army of the Republic Parade (Union Army celebration), held in downtown Marietta, is seen here around 1912. (Courtesy of John Patterson.)

Gus Coleman, champion of the Black Race Car Drivers in the South, is pictured here in Marietta, *c.* 1922. (Courtesy of the Georgia Department of Archives and History.)

This picture of shanty houses dates from around 1950. The houses are located in a black area of Marietta known as Baptist Town. (Courtesy of Hardy Studio, Marietta, Georgia.)

This scene shows groundbreaking ceremonies, c. 1948, for the first black hospital located on Montgomery Street in Marietta. The hospital was a county-wide project originated by the Men's Ideal Club. The hospital was closed after Kennestone Hospital was opened in 1951. (Courtesy of Powerpointe Archives.)

Despite poll tax requirements, literacy tests, and threats of violence, black people in Marietta are seen here lining up in front of the Cobb County courthouse waiting to register to vote. The Georgia Democratic primary was held on July 17, 1946, and black participation denied Eugene Talmadge the popular vote, though he won the majority of the county unit votes. (Courtesy of Hardy Studio, Marietta, Georgia.)

"Mr. Posey," a nickname given to him by the local children, rode his bull through Marietta daily. He is seen here on Church Street in Marietta, c. 1909. (Courtesy of John Patterson and Powerpointe Archives.)

The Kennesaw Train Depot is pictured above around 1870. Many black families would travel from Kennesaw to Marietta and on to Atlanta by train. (Courtesy of the Georgia Department of Archives and History.)

Louise Henry Burford and her mother, Mrs. Peggy Henry, sit at home, c. 1948. Both women were leaders in Marietta's black community. Louise Henry Burford was a former teacher at the city's colored school, Lemon Street. She later became church clerk at Zion Baptist. Peggy Henry taught Sunday school classes at the church for many years. (Courtesy of the Georgia Department of Archives and History.)

Emma Tanner of Kennesaw is pictured here in Kennesaw, *c.* 1920. (Courtesy of Powerpointe Archives.)

Mrs. Knox is pictured here in Kennesaw, *c.* 1920. (Courtesy of Juanita Byrd and Powerpointe Archives.)

Beullah Fowler, photographed in Marietta, *c.* 1940, was a relative of prominent businessman A.S. Fowler. She attended Morris Brown College in Atlanta. (Courtesy of Powerpointe Archives.)

Ernestine Jackson of Marietta and a friend enjoy a day of shopping on Peachtree Street in Atlanta, *c.* 1940s. (Courtesy of Ernestine Jackson.)

The National Travelers of Marietta was a popular gospel group in Marietta and Kennesaw during the 1940s and 1950s. (Courtesy of Juanita Byrd and Powerpointe Archives.)

Lettie Roberta Williams was the first black librarian in Cobb County and the first black woman in the county to join the army during World War II. (Courtesy of John Patterson.)

Kennesaw resident Ellis Bostic, a pastor and a descendant of one of the founding fathers of Sardis Baptist Church, worked at the Atlanta Army Depot during the Korean War. He received superior award performance certifications for innovative ideas that saved time and money on production. (Courtesy of Ellis Bostic and Powerpointe Archives.)

Juanita Byrd of Kennesaw shares four pictures of her father's brothers and sisters. The Daniel siblings were born and raised in Kennesaw. *Left:* This unidentified member of the Daniel family, photographed around 1920, died at a young age. (Courtesy of Juanita Byrd and Powerpointe Archives.) *Right:* An unidentified member of the Daniel family is seen in this picture, *c.* 1920. (Courtesy of Juanita Byrd and Powerpointe Archives.)

Left: Mary Daniel is seen here in a photograph dating from around 1930. (Courtesy of Juanita Byrd and Powerpointe Archives.) *Right:* Pictured here is John Daniel, *c.* 1930. (Courtesy of Juanita Byrd and Powerpointe Archives.)

BEAUMONT SCHOOL OF VOCATIONAL NURSING
CLASS OF MARCH 12, 1959
MRS. GLORIA JOHNSON, R.N., TEACHER

Mary Summerour (second row, second from the left) used to travel from Kennesaw to Atlanta to attend Beaumont School of Nursing. She is still providing nursing care to family and friends today. (Courtesy of Mary Summerour and Powerpointe Archives.)

Ten

A DEDICATION TO A KENNESAW HISTORIAN

"I never listened to that old saying, children are meant to be seen and not heard. As a boy, I would ask the grown ups questions about Black folks in Kennesaw, and they would tell me their stories."
—Alfred Jackson

In this photograph, Alfred Jackson, aged three years old, poses with his parents, *c.* 1929. Alfred, the son of Fred and Eros Lee Standifer Jackson, was born in Monticello, Georgia, in 1926. Alfred's parents moved to Kennesaw in 1928 to join his grandparents who were living there at the time. As a child, Alfred wanted to know about the history of black people of Kennesaw. He would ask his grandparents, neighbors, and sometimes strangers, making a mental record of everything that was said to him. A respected authority on black history in Kennesaw, Mr. Jackson has been invited to speak before the Kennesaw Historic Preservation Society and has been called on by Kennesaw State College professors to share his knowledge with their students. Mr. Jackson, a member of Mt. Zion AME Church in Kennesaw, has been the historian of the church for over 25 years. His commitment to family and the community has been immeasurable.

Alfred Jackson is photographed with his mother (left) and relatives at a family gathering, *c.* 1940. (Courtesy of Alfred Jackson.)

Eros Lee Standifer Jackson, father of Alfred Jackson, is seen here around 1950 at a Lockheed Union picnic. (Courtesy of Alfred Jackson.)

ACKNOWLEDGMENTS

Thanks go to my heavenly Father who is the guiding force of my life. Special thanks go to my husband, Brian E. Lassiter, for your encouragement. I appreciate all of your support. I thank my daughter Nia, for your understanding, while Mommie worked on her book. To my mother, Ursula H. Shelton, and my two cousins, Mike Clark and Eugene Roberts, I thank you for trailing the "back" roads of Kennesaw and Marietta with me. I extend special thanks to the following: the eldest member of the Jackson line, "Willie Bell Hall Johnson," her children, Neda and Billy, and grandson Dana; my mother and father-in-law, Mr. and Mrs. Cleveland Lassiter, and my brothers Bradley, Keith, Waytus, Roland, and Stevie for your encouragement and support; my father, Waytus C. Shelton Sr., who was supportive of my efforts; and my grandmother Lillian Lucille Shelton, who has been an inspiration throughout the years. Thanks go to my nephews Kharey and Mandi, nieces Cadeidra and Averi, sister and brother-in-law Mr. and Mrs. Clayton, and sisters-in-law Donna and Detra. I would also like to thank the many contributors who took the time to help make this project possible. They are as follows: Alfred Jackson; Aunt Ernestine Jackson; Attorney Vernon Slaughter; Ruby Haley; Reverend and Mrs. Byrd; Mr. and Mrs. Hanley; Rev. Ellis Bostic; Lula Rachael; cousin Reginald Kemp; Mary Summerour; cousin Harriet E. Scott; cousin Muriel J. Booker; Rev. Gabriel S. Hardeman and Henry Posh of the Turner Chapel AME; Rev. D.W. Jacobs of the Turner Theological Seminary; Mrs. Claudia McGuire; cousin Robert Jackson; cousin Alexander Jackson Jr.; cousin Ella Mae Jackson; Dr. Constance Carter of the Auburn Avenue Research Center; Juliet Dobbs Blackburn-Beamon DA; Alice Falls; Percy Price; cousin Jimmy Roberts; Mr. Gordon Belts of the National Model Railroad Association; Bridgette Eppinger Greene; "amazing" Rosa Andrews; cousin John Patterson; Herman "Skip" Mason; Betty Gillis of the Marietta City Schools; Barbara Duncan Ph.D. of the Museum of the Cherokee Indian; Katie White, Cindy Byrd, and Ingrid Patterson at Arcadia Publishing; and the nice people at the Georgia Department of Archives and History and the Federal Archives.

BIBLIOGRAPHY

Scott, Thomas Allan. "Cobb County, Georgia, 1880–1900: A Socioeconomic Study of an Upper Piedmont County." The University of Tennessee, Ph.D., 1978.

Elgin, Peggie R. "Marietta City Schools 1892–1992: Centennial Celebration." Marietta School Foundation, copyright pending.

Angell, Stephen Ward. *Bishop Henry McNeal Turner and African-American Religion in the South.* Knoxville: The University of Tennessee Press, 1992.

Pomerantz, Gary M. *When Peachtree Meets Sweet Auburn: The Saga of Two Families and the Making of Atlanta.* New York: Lisa Drew/Scribner, 1996.

Temple, Sarah Blackwell Gober. *The First Hundred Years: A Short History of Cobb County, In Georgia.* Atlanta: Walter W. Brown Publishing Company, 1935.

Young, Henry J. *Major Black Religious Leaders: 1755–1940.* Abingdon: The Parthenon Press at Nashville Tenn, 1977, 1979.

Fraizer, E. Franklin. *The Negro Church in America.* New York: Schocken Books, 1964.

Graebner, William and Leonard Richards, eds. "Images of The Nation's Past." The American Record. Volume One. Alfred A. Knopf Inc., 1982.

Mason, Herman "Skip." *Images of America: Black Atlanta in the Roaring Twenties.* Charleston: Arcadia Publishing, 1997.

Blankenship, Bob and Guion Miller Roll "Plus." *Of Eastern Cherokee East & West of the Mississippi 1909.* Cherokee Roots Publication, 1994.

Millard, Janet M. *A Woman's Place: 52 Women Of Cobb County, Georgia 1850–1981.* Cobb: Marietta Girls Club, 1981.

Dale, Everett Edward. *Gaston: Cherokee Cavaliers.* University of Oklahoma Press, 1995.

Other Sources

Georgia Archives: Microfilm: Census Records 1870–1940; Agricultural Census Records 1880–1910; Marriage and Death Records; Cobb Counties Tax Digest for 1907, 1908, 1909; Vanishing Georgia Collection

National Archives: 1909 Guion Miller Cherokee Applications; 1898 Dawes Applications

Cobb County Deed Office: Deed records from 1870–1934

Marietta Museum of History: Funeral Home History; Jackie Phillips Post Card Collection

Museum of the Cherokee Indian, Cherokee, NC